A PRACTICAL PRIMER ON PRAYER

by
Dorothy C. Haskin

MOODY PRESS
CHICAGO

Printed in the United States of America

The Reason for This Book

"After this manner therefore pray ye."—Matthew 6:9

SHALL I PRAY aloud or silently? Must I always kneel when I talk to God? Is it reverent to pray at odd moments? How should I begin a prayer?

These and a hundred other questions clamored for answers when I, at twenty-seven years of age, accepted Christ as my Saviour and began really to pray.

True, I had *repeated* prayers as a child, couplets which I had been taught; and in times of stress I had *cried,* "God, if there is a God, prove Thyself by helping me out of this trouble!"

Both are forms of prayer, the same as drinking from a bottle is eating to a baby; but they did not satisfy the one eager to know the Lord.

I read many excellent books which inspired

me and encouraged me to pray, but they did not answer my simple questions about the ABC's of praying.

Nor, as I learned later, was I the only one with childlike questions about prayer. As I taught in the church Bible school and as I sought to win others to my Lord, questions similar to and simpler than mine were raised. I could and did tell my own experiences in answer, but I longed for a simple book which I might place in their hands.

I have written this book, therefore, for the young Christian of any age who wants practical answers to the what, when, and how of prayer.

* * *

Contents

Pray for great things,
Expect great things,
Work for great things,
But above all, pray.

—REUBEN ARCHER TORREY

1

Praying in Public

"Many were gathered together, praying."
Acts 12:12

"IT IS EASY for him to pray but hard for me" is the thought that often comes when someone is heard to pray in public. But surely it wasn't easy for that one the first time. That experience is never easy.

I remember the first time I was asked to join a group for prayer. It was when I was attending the Bible Institute of Los Angeles. A noon-hour prayer meeting was held to encourage the students to pray for missionaries. I greatly admired the girl who was in charge of this group, so when she asked me to join the group, I did—to please her.

I had never prayed before in front of others, and a sharp pain came into the pit of my stomach when I knelt with the girls. The leader handed me a list of missionaries with their requests written after their names. We were to pray in turn. When my turn came, it came. I could not back out.

I peeked at the name and request of the first missionary on my list, closed my eyes, mumbled a prayer, peeked at another name, and so on, until I had named the last request. What a relief that was!

This group met each week. At first, my praying was probably not truly "in the Spirit"; but as the semester progressed, I conquered my nerve until I could pray in front of people without being at all conscious of their presence.

Because praying is spiritual, most people think it is like magic, a sort of "presto-chango, there it is"! Others think it is a gift and wish that God would give it to them. And still others, because requests are so common in spoken prayers, think that asking is all there is to prayer.

Spiritual things, however, follow the same laws as the physical; and prayer, being truly spiritual, needs practice to be developed. Even the disciples realized that a man had to be taught to pray. They asked, "Lord, teach us to pray" (Luke 11:1). Let us, therefore, begin our thinking on prayer with the understanding that one must learn to pray.

The only opportunity that the average Christian has to pray with others is in the young people's meeting or in the midweek service.

Often a person who has been a Christian for only a short time goes to one of these services, wanting and planning to take part in the prayer time. He may even make a false, dry-throated start or two, in between the easy-sounding prayers of the "regulars"; and then, just as he's gulped again and made ready, the leader closes the prayer period.

The easiest and best way for you to lose this feeling of self-consciousness when praying in a group is to pray aloud and often when alone with the Lord. Then, when you pray in public, the sound of your voice will not frighten you. It will seem natural and the presence of others will not bother you.

Christians even make a mistake in praying silently when they are alone. Jesus undoubtedly spoke His prayers. Otherwise, how would John have been able to record the high-priestly prayer of John 17? And when Jesus was in the garden of Gethsemane, He "fell on his face and prayed, saying . . ." (Matthew 26:39).

If Christ prayed aloud when He was in distress, shouldn't we follow His example and pray audibly when we are alone with God?

Here is another little hint which will help you. When you are alone, before you begin to pray, read one of the Psalms or any other favorite chapter of Scripture aloud. Then you will find it natural to slip into spoken prayer.

After you have become used to the sound of your own voice, the next battle to be won is over the feeling that others beside God are listening to you. This can only be won by concentrating on God, by thinking of Him so completely that you forget the others.

There is a story told of a man who was asked to lead in prayer, but who replied, "Please excuse me. I couldn't pray in front of others."

"Sir, you are to speak to your Master and not to them," was the answer. "And my Bible tells me He is not so critical and censorious as men are."

Another thing which bothers some people is the belief that their prayers must be extemporaneous, even though they are told ahead of time that they will be asked to lead in prayer. This is not true. In fact, they might well consider what they are going to say.

If you were asked to address a king in public, you would certainly give thought to what you were going to say. Why not give thought then when you are to speak to the Creator of heaven and earth, the only true God and Potentate?

Prayers are often said to be a blessing themselves to the listeners; and yours will be more of a blessing if instead of groping for words, you endeavor to express your highest thoughts.

Let us consider the different parts of a public prayer. For instance, there is the title by which we shall address God. I have taken quiet delight in noticing how various people address the Almighty.

It is not necessary always and only to address God as "Our Father." Why not think before deciding which title you will use? Many are permissible.

"Our Lord and our God." "Gracious and ever loving Father."

Dr. Walter Wilson speaks of Him as "Our lovely Lord." Our lovely Lord! How that title makes one dwell upon thoughts of His loveliness! Two or three times I tried using it, but since it did not come naturally, I stopped.

Once I heard a sailor pray, "Dear God, sir." That was natural to him. He had been trained to say "Sir" to those he respected.

You should use the title which best expresses your feeling toward God, and there are many to choose from; however, "Almighty God, our Father," is perhaps the most expressive. It has the combined thought that He is the ruler of heaven and earth and also our Father.

The Lord instructed us to say, "Our Father." The Scriptures tell us, too, "Ye have received the Spirit of adoption, whereby we cry, Abba, Father" (Romans 8:15).

Another excellent way to begin a public prayer is with a Psalm of praise. A good choice, for instance, would be the Eighth Psalm, which begins, "O Lord, our Lord, how excellent is thy name in all the earth!" Or how about a few verses from Psalm 103?

Always, before you mention your petitions, say a few words of thanksgiving or praise; but do not start by saying, "We come into Thy presence." This is not true.

You have not been out of the presence of God. As the Scripture reminds us, "Whither shall I go from thy Spirit? Oh whither shall I flee from thy presence? If I ascend up into heaven, thou art there: if I make my bed in hell, behold, thou art there" (Psalm 139:7,8).

We are always in the presence of God. If we live each moment conscious of His presence, we shall not have to readjust our mental attitude when we begin to pray, but we shall pray to the

One we have been silently including in our every thought and conversation.

Probably the best way to begin a prayer is with a grateful mention of Christ's death on the cross, "For through him we both have access by one Spirit unto the Father" (Ephesians 2:18).

In the body of your prayer, do learn to address the Deity as "Thou." It may sound stilted to you, but it has become a form of respect.

"You" is the commonly used form of the pronoun. "Thou" is really the intimate form, suggesting family relationship. Both were formerly used in English; and although we have dropped "thou" from our everyday speech, several other languages still have two forms for the pronoun "you."

Stay then with the Old English "Thou" and its forms. You will be both reverent and right.

Why not take a small slip of paper and list the requests you wish to make in your prayer? Do not misunderstand me. I don't mean for you to write out your prayers as some do. That may make praying stilted and may result in one's reading a prayer instead of praying.

We who are plain, average Christians with no one but God to please need not write our prayers. If we should forget what we want to say, that is all right. We can just stop, and the service is not disrupted. I merely meant for you to make a short list of the things you wanted especially to remember. In time and with training you will not need even that, but rather, only a little forethought.

There will be times when you cannot even make a list, for without warning someone will ask you to lead in prayer. This is your opportunity to praise the Lord for His many benefits. "Oh, that men would praise the Lord for his goodness, and for his wonderful works to the children of men!" (Psalm 107:31). Praise Him for His bountiful goodness, His gracious provision for His own, the privilege of living in a country of free worship, and the privilege of prayer. There are so many things for which to thank the Almighty that a grateful heart could pray on indefinitely.

After these words of praise, ask Him to bless the meeting, the message, those present, those absent and those ill or in special need. Pray for whatever special petitions may have been mentioned, then close.

Be careful to close your prayer in the name of the Lord Jesus. We do not have sufficient merit of our own so God will answer our prayers. He has promised to answer only the prayers made in Christ's name. "Whatsoever ye shall ask in my name, that will I do, that the Father may be glorified in the Son" (John 14:13).

The word "amen" means "so be it." We use it at the end of our prayers to mean that we accept God's answer, whether it be "yes" or "no."

Public prayer at the beginning of a meeting is for a definite purpose and should not be long. You are only to ask the Lord's blessing on the meeting.

Because a person takes a long time to pray, it does not necessarily follow that he has prayed for more than the person who has prayed a shorter prayer. A long prayer sometimes consists of a greater number of words without greater spirituality. Our Lord answered short prayers. When a woman prayed, "Lord, help me," He granted her request. When Peter walked on the water and became frightened, he cried, "Lord, save me." And the Lord did save him.

Spiritual pride may creep in with the ability to pray for a long time, and we should forego that tendency when praying before non-Christians. Prayer is apt to be boring to the person who is not a Christian, and in public meetings there are usually some present who are not Christians. We must consider them, because Scripture says of Paul, "I am made all things to all men, that I might by all means save some"

(I Corinthians 9:22). We should live up to that principle, hoping for the same privilege of winning some to Christ.

There is a story told about Moody and long public prayers. It is said that he was at a meeting where the person asked to make the opening prayer prayed on and on. So Moody arose and announced a hymn to be sung while the brother finished his prayer.

We should also consider the one who does not have the spiritual strength to pray long prayers. Our lengthy prayer might so embarrass him that he would hesitate to pray a shorter prayer.

Long prayers have their place in the Christian life; but they are to be prayed in our private devotions or with those of equal spiritual interests. This is true not only in public meetings, but also in prayer groups. If those in the group would pray shorter prayers, more people would be encouraged to take part.

Sometimes you will be in a group where the first person mentions all the requests. When that happens, the others in the group usually feel flat, as if there were no further reason to pray, even though they want to pray. I know of no remedy, since anyone in a prayer group is privileged to include all the requests if he wishes. But when that happens, you can always pray,

"Dear Lord, Thou hast heard the prayer. I add my voice and heart's desire to these requests."

Perhaps the best way to encourage different people to take audible part in a prayer group is for the leader to begin by asking different ones to volunteer to pray about certain requests.

Are you troubled about what you should do when someone else is praying? This used to bother me. I felt that it was impolite to listen when someone was talking to God; but if I didn't listen, my mind wandered. I didn't know what to do until one summer when I was a counsellor at a teen-age conference. One of my duties was attendance at a prayer group of the counsellors. The woman in charge was a highly respected spiritual leader of young people. I knew that she listened when others prayed because she said "amen" aloud whenever she agreed with what was said. I thought that whatever she did must be right.

Since then I listen to what is being prayed; and according to the custom of the group, I say "amen" either aloud or to myself, if I agree. I find this increases the spirit of united prayer.

There are times when the person who is praying mumbles to such an extent that you can't hear what he is saying. You feel, as the Scripture says, "If the trumpet give an uncertain sound, who shall prepare himself to the battle?" (I Corinthians 14:8). But prayer time is precious. Don't waste it. Pray silently whatever you think should be prayed at that time.

Sometimes no one prays aloud. Don't let the silence make you nervous. It does bother most people, and it used to affect me that way until I heard Dr. Louis Evans explain that silence has a part in prayer. Perhaps more people are actually praying during a time of silence than when someone is praying aloud. And you can always use the silence to present quietly an extra petition of your own.

Another difference that you will notice in Christian groups is that in some churches the people sit during prayer whereas in others they kneel and in still others everyone stands.

This is because churches follow different customs. The various ways are mentioned in the Bible. Mark 11:25 says "When ye stand praying." Psalm 95:6 says, "Let us kneel before the Lord, our maker." In I Kings we read that Elijah sat when he prayed. There is no set rule.

Scripture also says, "I will therefore that men pray everywhere, lifting up holy hands" (I Timothy 2:8). Only a few churches follow that instruction.

The important thing is that the position

should not make the praying one conscious of his body. Standing tires those who are not used to it. A sitting position puts the speaking organs in a cramped position. Kneeling is most frequently chosen, because the very position of the body expresses humility before the Almighty.

Most people close their eyes when they pray. They do so to shut out the things of the world. It helps to focus attention upon God, but it is not necessary when you are alone. Some day, stand alone on a hilltop beside a leafy tree, with the azure sky above and the wind on your face; the presence of God will be so real that it will not be necessary for you to close your eyes. You will be conscious only of Him and of His loveliness.

As long as we are discussing the technicalities of prayer, there is a bad habit about which I should like to warn you. Do not constantly repeat the Lord's name. Some people place it between every sentence as though it were a period. We would not naturally use a person's name that often in conversation. Sometimes, when this is done, the listener subconsciously listens for the repetition of the name and thus loses the spirit of prayer.

The same is true of the sound "uh." The constant repeating of sounds or words is merely a nervous habit that can be broken or even prevented with a little thought and effort. It is a test of our unselfishness to make our public prayers attractive to those who listen.

Several times we have discussed considering others when we pray. Let us admit at this point that it is possible to consider people too much when we pray. Prayer is always *to* God; yet some people pray *at* others.

Sometimes even valued servants of God, when they complete their messages and begin to pray, address a few sentences to the Almighty and then start to pray their message over again. You can sense when they stop talking to God and start praying at the congregation. If you can sense it, so can others, especially the non-Christians, and the spirit of prayer is lost.

Some people even pray *to others.* They use prayer as a means of giving out information about their work or the needs of the work. Or they may say things in their prayer about the people who are listening, things that they would not otherwise have the courage to say.

Still others yield to the temptation to pray showy prayers, hoping to impress others. We can only ask God to forgive them for abusing the precious privilege of prayer. Let us check our own spirit to see that we are not tempted to do the same thing. We should never pray anything in public that we do not mean from the depth of our hearts.

And it is possible to pray in public from the depth of the heart only if prayer is made daily, constantly, and worshipfully. Then you will be so accustomed to praying that you can pray naturally in public and your prayer will be a blessing.

God's Temple: A Prayer

O love divine, O matchless grace,
That Thou shouldst give me, Lord, a place
Within Thy temple fair,
Whose wondrous beauty, jewels bright,
Make not a perfect building quite
Without my humble share!

I would not make it my concern
On fretted arch or lofty dome
Conspicuous place to hold;
But though a lowly spot I fill,
With loving heart to work Thy will,
A perfect stone to mold.

And O, dear Lord, inspire my breast
With holy zeal to build my best
On Christ, the Cornerstone,
That in my own appointed place
The light of heaven may show rare grace
In what my hands have done!

And when shall come that last great day,
And all that's false must pass away
In fire's consuming test,
O may my building, wrought through Thee,
Stand fast; my glorious guerdon be
To share Thy heavenly rest!

—EMILY S. STRONG

2

The Key to Prayer

"We will give ourselves continually to prayer."
—Acts 6:4

HAVING REALIZED that the secret to public prayer is one's private prayer life, let us consider it. What does one do when alone with God? Do most Christians even have a quiet time with God each day?

No one will ever know the tremendous battles Christians fight to keep their quiet time. People seldom talk about these things. But oh, it is so easy to stop praying and to be too busy to read our Bibles! "What is the difference?" we think. "Who will know?"

As a matter of fact, others will know, because those who pray ask their questions of God, while those who neglect prayer are always asking others, "Why did this happen to me?" It takes only a half hour's conversation with a Christian for one with perception to sense that Christian's spiritual condition. "Out of the abundance of the heart, the mouth speaketh."

Some people live a full, rich Christian life, while others who name His name have a meager Christian spirit.

Because keeping one's quiet time with God is a battle and is the place where Satan attacks the Christian most frequently, let us consider some reasons for its importance.

Suppose you don't keep your quiet time, what will happen to you? There are many such Christians. God doesn't strike them dead. They manage to go along in the same old rut. That's it—they go along in the same old rut. They become second-rate, third-rate, tenth-rate Christians. They are Christians with no testimony, Christians who make the non-beliver say, "If he's a Christian, I don't want to be one." Don't you want to be a better testimony than that for your Master?

This is a day and age when we hear a good deal about people who are frustrated and who have inferiority complexes. Unfortunately, there are Christians who are frustrated and who also have complexes. They are the ones who do not keep their quiet time, for if they faithfully knelt in His presence, He would give them an abundant life—not in things, nor in the world—but in

Himself. "If any man thirst, let him come unto me, and drink. He that believeth on me, as the scripture hath said, out of his belly shall flow rivers of living water" (John 7:37,38). He would show them that having His love is alone sufficient to keep any of His children from feeling inferior. "I can do all things through Christ which strengtheneth me" (Philippians 4:13).

Nor is the Christian who neglects his quiet time prepared when trouble comes. It comes to all of us, and at best it is hard to endure; but the Christian without the devotional habit not only suffers but also is confused and bewildered. Martin Luther said, "Were it not for tribulation in my life, I should not understand Scripture"; but most of us feel, "Were it not for Scripture, I should not understand trouble."

Physical health and spiritual health are alike in many ways. It is easier to fight a cold if you are healthy, and it is easier to fight temptation if you are spiritually up to par. And the way to keep spiritually fit is by means of that daily dozen with the Bible and prayer.

It isn't easy for the Christian to live up to the highest. He has to look often into His Master's face to keep his aspirations up to the highest notch. Too many times when the desire of the flesh is strong, when the sacrifice of tithing seems very great, when the spirit rebels at being meek, only the daily reading of the Scripture will put steel into the Christian's consecration.

It is important to keep our quiet time, too, because God needs leaders. There is much work to be done by those who will serve Him, not only in the pulpit or on the mission field, but also in your block. Wherever you are, God placed you there, making you responsible for that portion of "the field."

We are to be privileged to throw our crowns at His feet; therefore, it would be wonderful to have some to throw. But how can we have any if we have not kept our quiet time and thus have not known what He would have us do and say to earn those crowns?

It is surprisingly easy to skip one's quiet time. Just stay up a little later at night, press a dress you hadn't planned to wear, or spend your time on the telephone. God will not compel you to grow spiritually. Some children have to be taught to eat, and some Christians have to be taught to eat spiritual food. "Thy words were found, and I did eat them; and thy word was unto me the joy and rejoicing of mine heart: for I am called by thy name, O Lord God of hosts" (Jeremiah 15:16).

Once you are convinced that it is a matter of

spiritual life or death that you have your devotions—then your problem is *time.* Believe me, you will never *find* the time; you will have to *take* the time. It has been said: "If you are too busy to pray, you are *too busy!*"

You and I think that we are busy. Let us consider some men who were really busy and see if they had time to be quiet before God.

John Wesley preached 44,000 sermons in his lifetime. He traveled on horseback and by carriage 290,000 miles. He wrote an English dictionary; prepared grammars in Hebrew, Latin, Greek, French and English; wrote several volumes on theology, history, philosophy and medicine; and edited a fifty-volume set of books. Yet he had time for daily Bible study.

For two years while General Sir William Dobbie was Governor of Malta, he was under almost continuous bombing by a nearby powerful enemy with plenty of bombs; but though he was busy helping with the wounded, he also held Bible classes nightly for his officers and men.

Surely there was no one busier than General Douglas MacArthur, head of the army of occupation in Japan; yet he said: "However tired I may be, I never go to bed without reading a portion of this book—the Bible."

Luther is said to have spent three hours a day

in prayer. The busier he was, the more time he felt he *had* to spend with God.

We human beings do the things which we think are important. If we think it important that we look attractive to others, we devote time to our bodies. If we think it is important to spend time with God, we will do it. Jesus said, "Seek first the kingdom of God." If we truly want to obey Him, we will find time to pray *first.*

Those who are not Christians but who have succeeded in other lines have learned the necessity of putting first things first. A noted young concert artist was asked the secret of her mastery of the violin.

"Planned neglect," she replied and then explained: "There were many things which used to demand my time. When I went to my room after breakfast, I made my bed, straightened the room, dusted, and did whatever seemed necessary. When I finished my work, I turned to my violin practice. That system failed, however, to accomplish what I should on the violin, so I reversed things. I deliberately planned to neglect everything else until my practice period was complete. And that program of planned neglect is the secret of my success."

The best time—truly, the *only* time for me—to

have our worship period is in the morning. Can you give less than the freshest, brightest moments to God? Shouldn't we all say with the Psalmist, "My voice shalt thou hear in the morning, O Lord; in the morning will I direct my prayer unto thee and will look up" (Psalm 5:3)?

I think the custom of saying our prayers at night arose from the fact that as children most of us were taught to say the "Now I lay me" prayer before we went to sleep. It has become a habit to many people. I know several worldly, sinful people who still repeat the Lord's prayer or some childhood prayer before they go to sleep.

Let me tell you of Kohila, a young Hindu nurse who worked in an orphanage. "Beware of saying 'I have no time to read my Bible and pray'; but rather say, 'I have not bothered to discipline myself to do those things,' " was what she wrote on a piece of paper and hung over the sink where she washed bottles for the nursery. She had to rise at five-thirty in the morning to read her Bible and pray. If she could do that, so can we!

"Whatever is your best time in the day, give that to communion with God," was the advice of Hudson Taylor, founder of the China Inland Mission, to one of the first women missionaries to China. No one ever woke up in a Chinese inn where Hudson Taylor was but that he was already awake and praying.

The men God has used have always given their first moments to Him. Sunrise always found David Livingstone on his knees before God. He even died on his knees while praying in the heart of Africa.

Jewelers say that the best time to wind a watch is in the morning. It is certainly the best time to wind one's life by prayer. In the morning we ask the Lord's blessing *before* we do things instead of *after*. We then face the problems of the day with a quieter, more peaceful spirit if we rise early enough to have our devotion first.

If you find, however, that when you tumble out of bed and on your knees, you go back to sleep, then you might pray standing up until you are sure you are fully awake.

Or try George Mueller's system. He dressed before he had his devotions. You will remember George Mueller as the Englishman from the last century who supported hundreds of orphans and many missionaries on faith.

The housewife may not be free to have her devotions until the door has closed behind the last person leaving the house; but then, despite the household tasks which clamor for her attention, she can with practice shut her eyes to them and seek God *first*.

Small children can be placed in a play-pen or, if older, can be trained to play quietly at this time. One woman used to put her apron over her head when she prayed so that the children would understand not to disturb her.

Frankly, the easiest way to get up in the morning is to go to bed early at night.

When Howard Guinness, missionary to China, decided, "From today the central thing in my life shall be prayer," he realized he would have to go to bed earlier than was his custom. He was a student at that time and often stayed up late studying. To solve his problem, he first decided upon a rising hour. Then, working back counter-clockwise to allow for the required hours of sleep, he determined the hour when he must close his books and go to bed. That schedule became the habit of his life.

What keeps you up late, anyway? A boy friend? A book? Whatever it is, you have unconsciously put that thing ahead of the Lord. Could you stay up late if you knew that by so doing you would miss seeing someone you loved greatly? No. Then pray that God will give you a great love for Himself.

Meanwhile, if you have trouble getting up,

here is a sure cure. Promise yourself, as did Leland Wang, noted and loved Chinese evangelist, "No Bible, no breakfast!" After you have gone without breakfast a couple of times, you will get up in time for both.

And on that morning when you have to get up exceptionally early to meet a train, or if you oversleep, at least do this much: from a "Promise Box" or other collection of cards with verses printed on them, select a verse, put it in the mirror frame, and glance at it many times as you dress. It will turn your thoughts heavenward.

The most important thing is that you stick to whatever time you decide upon as best for you. "It is required in stewards that a man be found faithful" (I Corinthians 4:2).

Devotions may take a long time or a short time. Five minutes, a half hour, two hours. As a spark of life may be sustained upon a meager diet, so many a dwarfed spiritual life be sustained upon skimpy spiritual food. As more food gives one greater energy, so more time spent with the Lord gives one greater spiritual energy. Try taking a mental snapshot of yourself to decide how much strength your body would have if you ate only as often as you read God's Word.

All too often when we go into our prayer closets, our subconscious attitude is, "Lord, I have five minutes to spare. If Thou hast anything to say to me, say it quickly." We think we have so much to do!

God knows the value of your time. He knows what else you should or might be doing and exactly how important that thing is. The busier we are and the more valuable our time is the more choice it is to give Him.

"A calm hour with God is worth a whole lifetime with man," wrote Robert Murray McCheyne, a young Scottish preacher who was greatly used of God. Although he died in his twenty-ninth year, he was recognized as one of the great spiritual leaders of his day. His sermons and notes are still read by Christians to inspire them to a closer walk with God.

If you really want to know the Lord, you will have to spend time with Him; that is the key to the quiet time. You have to *want* to keep it.

The Cry of the Heart

Jesus, we kneel at Thy dear feet,
Because Thou bidst us come;
'Tis there we find a safe retreat,
Thy words will guide us home.

Thy pardoning grace is full and free,
And free Thy boundless love;
There is no other help but Thee,
Our Father, God, above!

Remove the pain and guilty fear
From our poor sinful hearts!
O, wipe away each bitter tear,
Thy healing grace impart!

Make us obedient to Thy will,
To shun the world and sin;
Lord, with Thy Holy Spirit fill
Our longing souls within!

When we the cross no longer bear,
When pilgrim life is o'er,
Set free from earthly sin and care,
We'll praise Thee evermore!

—Charlotte Mary Shey

3

God's Word in the Quiet Time

"Thou hast magnified thy word above all thy name."
—Psalm 138:2

NOW THAT WE'VE DECIDED to keep our quiet time, what shall we do in that time?

Devotions should consist of reading the Bible and of prayer. A devotional book is sometimes helpful; but if something must be left out, that should be the one to be omitted, because such a book, of course, contains merely the thoughts of other men. Reading the Bible is most important, for that is God's very word to us.

It is surprising how many reverse this order. In a recent survey among juvenile delinquents 46 per cent of them prayed, but only 7 per cent of them read the Bible. This ought not to be, because praying is your talking to God, while the Bible is His talking to you; and it is more important that He talk to you than that you talk to Him.

How much the reading of God's message should mean to us! Unfortunately, many of us have grown too used to it. This is not true all over the world. Let me quote part of a letter from a missionary to the Nosu tribes in southwest China, and you will see how much God's Word means to those people.

"Last Saturday an old deacon came to us from his village fifty miles away and bought a New Testament. He did not return home that night. He sat on our doorstep and read and read until all his affections were coming out of his eyes in water. When I rose at daybreak to go to an outstation for a service, he was still there reading. When I returned, he was still in the same spot. Praise God for the Book!

"One outstation group waylaid my carriers and snatched a whole load of Testaments. 'Oh,' they said, 'we've waited for years for these. Tell the pastor all the money will be handed in within two weeks.' Strong men and boys have wept for joy as they have taken the Holy Book into their hands.

"Nothing has moved me so much in many years as this blessed sight of Nosu believers poring with rapturous wonder over the Word of the living God in their own tongue."

"A clean Bible—a lean Christian" was the

clever saying of Dr. William Evans, renowned Bible teacher, and there is truth in what he said. It is better to own a series of inexpensive Bibles that you feel free to mark than an expensive Bible, which you feel you must handle with care.

It is helpful for two reasons to mark a Bible. It makes you concentrate on what you are reading, and it helps you to find a special verse when it is needed again.

An interesting way to mark a Bible is to use a red pencil or a whole box of colored pencils. The different colors may be used for different subjects—red for salvation through the blood of Christ, yellow for the Holy Spirit, blue for heaven, green for earthly promises, etc. It is also helpful to keep a small card in your Bible to place under the pencil when marking. It will help you keep the line straight and neat.

Even a careless reading of God's Word is better than none; but if you wish to become familiar with the great truths of the Word, take a section, a chapter or more, and read the same passage every day for a week. Dr. G. Campbell Morgan, an outstanding Bible teacher in England, read the minor prophets more than forty times before he ever preached on them.

Let us pause right here to emphasize that merely reading the Bible is not enough for the

Christian. Scripture says, "*Study* to show thyself approved unto God, a workman that needeth not to be ashamed" (II Timothy 2:15). This does not mean reading the Bible as most of us do, but studying it until we actually know what it says.

The best way to study the Bible is by making a devotional notebook. It will become your own personal commentary. It should take you about three years to go through the Bible verse by verse; but if you do so, you will have a basic knowledge of its contents when you are finished.

Here are a few suggestions for your notebook.

You might outline the chapter. For instance:

John 1: 1-14 Introduction

John 1:15-34 The ministry of John the Baptist.

John 1:35-51 Calling the five. List the names.

Or you could write a a summary of the verses read. The meaning of a verse will become clearer to you if you put it in your own words.

It is true that when writing a summary, you will at times have to copy the actual words of the Bible, especially when quoting conversation. This may seem like mere copying, but it is more than that. The writing of words makes you pay closer attention to what is said and reveals new truths.

Here is an example. I was puzzled when I read in the Gospel of John of only Mary Magdalene at the empty tomb. I knew there had been several women who went to the tomb, and I wondered. It was not until I actually copied the words in John 20:2 that I noticed Mary's use of the pronoun "we," including the other women, and I saw that the passage was in harmony with the other gospels.

You may be interested in prophecy. It is interesting to list all the Old Testament scriptures which are mentioned in Matthew as fulfilled and then to look them up in the Old Testament. This method helps you to see the divine unity of the Old and New Testaments. It shows that all Scripture is related to Christ. "In the volume of the book, it is written of me" (Psalm 40:7). And the New Testament can be understood correctly only in the light of the Old Testament.

To be really at home in the Bible, you ought to study a map of the places mentioned and know the value of the different pieces of money. Why was it out of Jesus' way to go through Samaria? How much difference was there between the two sums owed in the parable of the unjust steward?

Most Bibles have maps and money tables in the back. You can check such helps as you read.

As you study the Bible, you will notice many references to the same subject, and you will want to start a list of topical references. In one section of your looseleaf notebook, list the headings which interest you; under them write the references and your conclusions.

For instance, there is Satan. Because in this day and age we are inclined to ignore him, it may surprise you to learn how much the Bible says of his power.

Another valuable topic is Christ's commandments. He says, "Ye are my disciples *if* ye keep my commandments." What are they? You might head a page "His Commandments" and as you find them, list them.

Or you may be interested in what Scripture has to say about prayer, the Holy Spirit, or even hell.

It will help you when you study the Bible, if you remember that Scripture, unlike any other book, has three meanings. First, the Book is historical. The incidents in it actually happened. Secondly, most of the verses refer to Christ, either by prophecy or type. "All things must be fulfilled which were written in the law of Moses and in the prophets and in the psalms, concerning me" (Luke 24:44). Lastly, there is a personal application. God still means what He said, and He means for you to obey.

Make this a rule in your Bible study—don't rush. Be content, if necessary, to study just one verse or to look up one cross reference. It is better to master a comma a day than to hurry through the Book and not know any of it.

If you want a guide for your study, the Christian magazine *His* offers an excellent one. It suggests that after you have read the Scripture, you ask yourself these questions:

"Is there any example for me to seek to follow by God's help?"

"Is there a command to be obeyed?"

"Is there a sin for me to avoid or forsake?"

"Is there a promise for me to claim; if so, what are its conditions?"

"What does this passage teach me (by illustration or statement) about Jesus Christ, God, myself, or His will for my life?"

"Is there something in this passage which should be my prayer for today?"

Also, in your Bible study, dare to be brave. When a question comes to you, write it down and pray for the answer. Many an answer will be found in another portion of Scripture. If the meaning of a verse is obscure, you may have to look in a commentary. If you can't afford to buy a commentary, try making your own by clipping the lesson helps from Sunday school lessons and pasting them into a scrapbook. (Paste them in the order of the books of the Bible.)

If you can afford a commentary, there is the one by *Jamieson, Fausset and Brown.* It is sensible, and yet it treats Jesus Christ and His death on the cross reverently. Sometimes when a verse says something you don't like, you look it up in the commentary. "Yes," agrees your commentator, "it does say that; but it is all right, and here's why." And the explanation follows. In searching the Scriptures we must be prepared to lose some of our preconceived ideas.

Surely, a study of the Bible includes memorizing some of the verses. Oh, how our lazy minds dislike to memorize! It is hard work, but suppose you set yourself to learn a verse each week—that's not so much. That way in a year's time you will know fifty-two verses.

One reason many people do not make a success of their memorizing is that they do not realize they must review and review the verses. In the first week, learn one verse. In the second week, review the first verse and learn one more and so on.

Keep a list of the verses you are supposed to

know and go over them each morning for your devotions. It would not be amiss sometimes to devote all of your quiet time to memorizing a verse. The reason God has so few effective witnesses is that so few people can actually quote the Word when they need it. Only a verse from the Bible settles an argument. Anything else you may say is still just your opinion, and the other person is entitled to his own opinion.

Our quiet time is sacred and should not become routine. Sometimes, instead of following your usual system of study, simply meditate upon the Word. Paul wrote to Timothy, "Meditate upon these things."

As one form of meditation, may I suggest that you select a Psalm or any other chapter of Scripture to read every day for a month. Read it in a low tone of voice so that you may concentrate on what you are reading. If you do that, you will find that your soul delights in the passage. Would you like to try the 103rd Psalm, or the 90th, or the 84th, for a starter?

Above all, ask the Lord, "What is Thy message for me today?" The American Bible Society prints a suggested Bible reading guide which says, "Search for the personal message in each day's passage for you. Your inner response to God's message is vital. When He condemns, bow penitently; when He offers help, place your hope on that assurance; when He commands, obey."

"Have you not often found that if you read the Bible consecutively, the passage which comes in due course will, somehow or other, prove to be as truly a lesson for the day as if it had been written on purpose to meet your case?" is the way Charles Haddon Spurgeon expressed this truth. Mr. Spurgeon was an outstanding Baptist evangelist in England during the nineteenth century, and his sermons are still read with delight by many Christians.

God will not say the same thing to you that He does to someone else. That is the mystery of the Book. But He will speak. If you find no message there, take a second look. It may be that you have not *wanted* to see it.

We must face the fact that all men are sinners, including you and me, and that even the best person in the world has some false ideas. Being a Christian calls for the remaking of the mind and personality to meet God's highest ideals. It is putting every thought and desire under the light of the Word. "Having therefore these promises, dearly beloved, let us cleanse ourselves from all filthiness of the flesh and spirit, perfecting holiness in the fear of God" (I Corinthians 7:1). If you grasp one truth a day, your opinions will in time reflect neither the world, nor tradition, nor your environment, nor even your minister, but the Lord.

Don't be discouraged if sometimes your Bible study seems dry. That is often true of the beginner who knows little of the Lord and His Word. It is like talking with a stranger; you have little in common with him and the conversation is apt to be dull. One outstanding Christian told me that when he first began to read the Bible daily, his reading was often so dry that he thought he was not learning anything during his study. But later when people asked him questions, he found that the Holy Spirit brought the Scripture to mind and that his blessing had been greater than he had realized.

My Prayer

Help me, O God, to dry each bitter tear;
Help me, O God, to banish every fear;
And when I find my pathway hard and drear,
Help me to know my Saviour still is near.

Help me to know that light can darkness rend;
Help me to see that sun and shadow blend;
Help me to feel Thou wilt Thine own defend,
And journey with me even to the end.

Grant me the strength to do each daily task,
My disappointment cheerily to mask;
And some fair morn in heaven's glow to bask—
These are the things, my God, I humbly ask.

—MYRA HEWSON MCINTIRE

4

Prayer in the Quiet Time

"Pray to thy Father."—Matthew 6:6

READING GOD'S WORD is only part of the Christian's quiet time. Another phase of it is praying to our Heavenly Father.

Let us always begin our prayer with praise and thanksgiving. God intended praise to be a large part of the Christian's worship. The Book of Psalms, longest in the Bible, is a book of worship and has one hundred fifty chapters, most of which are praise to God. "Praise is comely to the righteous."

Praise is different from thanksgiving. Thanksgiving is for a definite thing which we have received, but praise is for the fact that God is God. Praise Him that He gave His Son to die on the cross for your sins. Praise Him for the privilege of praying in Jesus' name. Praise Him for His Fatherhood. Praise Him! Praise Him!

After praise comes thanksgiving. We are all too prone to ask the Almighty for favors, but to be lax in thanking Him for them. How many times did you pray for that thing? Have you thanked Him that many times for granting your request? Search your heart and thank Him for His many blessings.

After your soul is flooded with gratitude to God, then make your petitions. What will you pray about? Everything! Jesus tells us not only to pray for big things, such as the filling of the Holy Spirit, but also for small things. We see that God answers lesser prayers as well because, when the man dropped the *borrowed* ax into the water, God made the iron to swim.

Isn't it wonderful that we have a God who is a Father and who is interested in everything which concerns us? "The Lord will perfect that which concerneth me" (Psalm 138:8).

The scope of prayer is narrowed only by the confines of our lives and desires. We can pray about anything to the God who with infinite attention to detail fashioned the insect and the star-flung sky.

If you want to be certain that your prayers will be answered, you must learn to claim promises. Search the Word for the things which God has promised to do and then ask Him to do them.

"It is a blessed way of praying, to pray upon a promise and to plead, 'Do as Thou hast said,' " is the way Robert Murray McCheyne words his encouragement to pray promises.

Here are a few promises that you may wish to pray.

For material care: "Give us this day our daily bread" (Matthew 6:11). "Bread shall be given him; his water shall be sure" (Isaiah 33:16). There are many bread promises, but I have found no cake promises. Cake is the extra goodness of the Lord.

For clothing: (Matthew 6:31-33)

For the salvation of loved ones: (II Peter 3:9)

For the salvation of a husband: (I Peter 3:1) (Please note the condition attached to the promise: the wife must be meek).

For the spiritual growth of loved ones: (Philippians 1:9-11)

For wisdom in making decisions: (James 1:5 and Isaiah 30:21). Please note the condition in the Isaiah promise.

For strength *in* or deliverance *out of* trouble: (Psalm 91:15 and Isaiah 43:2)

We cannot consider prayer without including faith, for faith is a very real part of prayer.

"When ye pray, believe." Does that seem hard to do? If so, here are George Mueller's rules for increasing your faith.

1. Carefully read the Word of God. (Romans 10:17)

2. Maintain an upright life and a good conscience. (Hebrews 10:22)

3. Do not shrink from opportunities where your faith may be tried. (I Peter 1:17)

4. When the hour of trial comes, do not work a deliverance for yourself. (Daniel 3:17)

All these rules are important, but I want to comment upon the last two. "Do not shrink from opportunities where your faith may be tried." This is so important. Unless your faith is tried, it will not grow. When the disciples asked the Lord, "Increase our faith," His answer included the thought that if one uses what he has, his faith will increase.

Time after time in Scripture we see the Lord testing a person's faith that it might grow. For instance, there is the time when the nobleman came to ask that his son be healed, as recorded in John 4; then there is the time when Jesus delayed answering the request of Mary and Martha for their brother's healing. If you will dare to pray for a definite request, your faith will grow.

Mueller's fourth point, "Do not work a deliverance of your own," is warning against a human temptation. Because we are afraid that God will not answer, we try frantically to solve our own problems. But God *will* answer. The thing is that He does not answer ahead of time, but *on* time.

I remember once when I was going to Bible school that I did not have carfare for the next day. I had faith until five o'clock in the evening; then I grew discouraged. But at seven o'clock a friend who owed me some money came and paid me!

Another way to increase your faith is to keep a section of your devotional notebook for prayer requests. When you pray for something, write it down with the date; then watch for the answer.

I remember vividly when I started mine. A close friend, for whose healing three of us had prayed earnestly, died. My faith tottered, and doubt taunted me that perhaps many other prayers had not been answered. I decided to keep books and see.

I bought a notebook; and as I prayed, I wrote down my request with the date and the verse if I was claiming a verse. Then I left space to write whether or not the prayer had been answered.

The first page records twelve known answers and three not granted, as far as I know.

The second page, fifteen known answers out of seventeen requests.

The third page, twenty-three known answers out of twenty-four requests.

The fourth page, fourteen known answers out of fifteen requests.

The fifth page, ten known answers out of eleven requests.

The sixth page, twelve known answers out of thirteen requests.

The seventh page, six known answers out of seven requests.

The eighth page, ten known answers out of twelve requests.

The figures themselves stagger one. Those prayers covered many things: the renting of a room, the grace to forgive, a new dress for Easter, a missionary speaker for a service, and prayers for others.

God forgave me for my lack of faith; and out of this experience came one of the greatest blessings of my life, the proof that He does answer prayer.

If you will keep a record of your prayers, your

prayer life will be improved in two ways. For one thing, it will weed out your prayers. As you write down requests, they will seem so petty and selfish that you will not pray about them.

Then, too, the list of answered prayers will increase your faith. When the devil tempts you to doubt, as he will, you can point to the pages and say, "God has answered before; He will answer again." It is an anchor for your faith in time of testing.

If faith is a necessary part of prayer, so is persistency. Jesus teaches this in the parable of the judge and the importunate widow. (Luke 18:1-8)

And why should we not persist in prayer? We are willing to persist in other matters. A good illustration of this is given by Isaac Page, for years a missionary to China under the China Inland Mission. When he was in China, a beggar used to stand at the door of his compound. Every time he saw Mr. Page—if it was once or a hundred times a day—he would beg, "One lone cash." A cash is a very small sum in China. But, rain or shine, hot or cold, time after time the beggar cried, "One lone cash! One lone cash!" Nothing ever stopped him.

Why should we not persist that much in our praying to God? Why not plead day after day for the salvation of a loved one? For laborers to be thrust out into the harvest field? For a life transformed by the Spirit?

But you object, "Suppose I do not feel like praying?" To that I can only answer that prayer is not a mood, but a duty. If we did only what we felt like doing, not much would be accomplished. Suppose a woman washed the dishes only when she was in the mood?

"True faith is prayer without feeling," was the conclusion of Francis Fenelon, outstanding Christian of the seventeenth century, whose small book entitled *Christian Perfection* is read often in these days by Christians who need help along the way.

"Pray hardest when it is hardest to pray" is the encouraging word of Charles H. Brent. And William Booth, founder of the Salvation Army, testified that, more often than not, he went to the place of prayer reluctantly, but that when he refused to give in to his feelings, God always blessed him.

Now that we have pointed out the duty of praying regardless of feeling, let us consider the different things which cause dryness in prayer, a state more common than most of us realize. Because people dislike to admit that they feel that way, the condition is seldom brought into the open and discussed. Sometimes the answer is simple.

Dryness may be caused by a slowing down of your growth. As human beings, we grow continuously; but the older we become, the less obvious is the growth. So it is spiritually; as we become adults in the Lord, we grow more slowly. A babe in Christ can often be seen to grow by "leaps and bounds," but the growth of a minister is seldom noticeable.

Or we may lack the desire to pray because our lives are untroubled. When life goes along smoothly and there is no emotional problem clutching at our hearts, we are inclined not to pray as ardently as when we are in trouble. I am afraid that is why many Christians have trouble. It is so easy for us to become self-satisfied and self-centered.

"Often our trials act as a thorn hedge to keep us in the good pasture, but our prosperity is a gap through which we go astray." Thus Charles H. Spurgeon expressed the need for trouble in the life of a Christian.

However, the cause of dryness in prayer may be deeper. It may be caused by sin.

Perhaps your sin was that you didn't obey the Word, and consequently you lost your taste for it. You "watered the Word." You said, "I don't think the verse means exactly that." For example, Scripture says, "Give no thought for tomorrow." But the woman who loves the world excuses herself: "We're supposed to take care of ourselves, though." She buys closetfuls of clothes and extra sets of dishes, saying, "If I don't, I won't have any." It may be that the Lord didn't want her to have so many things, but wanted her to devote herself to Him!

Or you make the excuse, "Tithing is Old Testament only." Are you sure? Look up Luke 11:42.

It may be that there has been sin against someone. Our prayer life is closely bound up with our relation to our fellow man, for God says, "When ye stand praying, forgive" (Mark 11:25). You cannot expect God to answer your prayer if you have an unforgiving spirit. "But," you argue, "God does not mean for me to forgive, because that person hurt my child." Unless a thing is unfair, there is nothing to forgive. You need only to remember that wicked men crucified Christ and that He forgave to know that God means for you too to forgive.

If you would enjoy fellowship with God, you must obey Him. He will bless you *afterwards.*

We even sin in this matter of confessing sin.

Our natural pride is so great that we dislike

to admit that we have done wrong. We seem to think that if we merely attempt to stop sinning, that is enough. But Scripture does not say, "If we stop sinning . . ." but rather, "If we *confess* our sins, he is faithful and just to forgive us our sins, and to cleanse us from all unrighteousness."

Perhaps you have drifted into unconfessed sin because you use what is called the "editorial we" in your prayers. You say, "Lord, *we* have sinned." You do that to lessen your own sense of guilt; but as long as you do it, you won't get close to God. It is like approaching Him in a crowd.

Instead, ask yourself: In what instance did *I* fail to obey God? Ask the Holy Spirit to direct your thoughts to any sin in your life. Read your Bible; and after each verse ask yourself, "Have I obeyed this?" God convicts of sin when the heart responds to His Word.

If sin has robbed the Christian of his blessing, two things are required of him. He must be right with both God and man. He must confess his sin to God and make restitution to the person wronged.

If you have wronged another, apologize. Don't hesitate to apologize. You may have the idea that making an apology will humiliate you, but it won't. It takes a big soul to have the grace to admit, "I was wrong." And here is a safe rule to follow in making restitution. Make it only as far as you have wronged. If the wrong was only in your heart, correct it there. If you have made an unkind remark, apologize to that person alone. But if you have gossiped, go to everyone to whom you have told the wrong story and correct it.

But we hope that your reluctance to pray is not caused by sin. Let us say it is merely that your mind wanders. Many Christians have faced this problem. Here is a suggestion made by Hudson Taylor, founder of the China Inland Mission:

"Regarding a wandering mind in prayer, I have found more help in praying aloud and praying while walking about—praying as to a present Lord—than in any other way."

Reading the Word will also stimulate your praying. Read a verse, then pause and pray. The Word will give vision to your praying by bringing to your mind friends and conditions which need prayer.

Try variety in your quiet time. Instead of reading your routine chapter a day, read only a verse and analyze it. Ask yourself: Am I really living this verse? For instance, "Thou shalt love the Lord thy God with all thy heart, and with all thy soul, and with all thy mind, and with all thy strength" (Mark 12:30). Does the Lord come first in your heart? Even ahead of your family? Is He the delight of your innermost being, or do you have secret ambitions in which He has no part? Does He dominate your mind, or do you think thoughts which by their very nature exclude Him? Do you actually give Him all your strength in service?

Or go to the other extreme and read a larger portion of the Bible than usual. Choose a book like Ephesians, Philippians, Colossians, or Philemon to read through at one sitting. You might once in a while even spend your quiet time reading a missionary magazine and thinking of the vastness of God's love, which encircles the whole world.

Vary your prayers too. One day pray for no one but yourself. Search your heart, humble yourself before the Lord, and dedicate yourself anew to living for Him. Let Him through His Spirit point out what He would take away from your life and what He would add to it.

Another day do not pray for yourself at all. Forget your own problems. You have already committed them to the Lord. Pray for others. Pray for your neighbors, mentally going from one house to another in your block, naming each member of the household. Or study a map of the world and pray for country after country, both the Christians and those who have never even heard of Jesus. Pray as the Holy Spirit brings names and conditions to your mind. Pray for those for whom you have never prayed before.

There are two ways to cure reluctance to be alone with God. One is to go down into the valley of the shadow of death, face the fact of the judgment seat of Christ, and come up to keep your quiet time. Few people live their lives with the surety of judgment always in view; but if you go through an illness which makes it real to you, then you will know the importance of being alone with God each day.

The other way is to fall in love with the Lord Jesus. Love for the Lord, like earthly love, does not come to all in the same way. With some, it is love at first sight. From the first moment they see Him, they fall at His feet, delighted with Him. Others grow slowly into knowing Him, into adoring Him. But whether this love rushes or creeps into your soul, when it comes, nothing can keep you from your quiet time and the joy of being with the Lover of your soul.

Wait on the Lord

My soul, wait only on the Lord,
Expecting nothing save from Him.
Rest all on His unfailing Word
Nor ever let thy faith grow dim.
Thine every need shall be supplied,
Thy heart's desires be freely given,
And no good thing shall be denied
The soul in harmony with heaven.

All human strength but disappoints,
Its wrecks along life's path are strewed;
But they who wait as God appoints
Shall daily find their strength renewed.
On eagles' wings of faith they rise
And far above earth's tumult sail,
They run, unwearied, toward the prize,
They walk, and neither faint nor fail.

However hopeless seems thy case,
Go spread it out before the throne;
And in His boundless, matchless grace,
Our God will make His power known.
Then in His strength go meet thy task,
Assured He bears with thee the load.
If great thy need, then largely ask;
All things are possible with God.

—Mrs. W. A. Vroman

5

Listen!

"Speak, for thy servant heareth."—I Samuel 3:10

NOW WE HAVE COME to the most solemn part of all our quiet time—God's talking to you! A very real part of your quiet time should be spent just being still before God—waiting, waiting for Him to speak.

We must come to the place where we cease to be concerned about ourselves or our feelings, where we are concerned only about God. We should cease to think of our quiet time as a means of bettering ourselves, of "feeling good" or getting a blessing, but as a time of finding Him. "When thou saidst, Seek ye my face; my heart said unto thee, Thy face, Lord, will I seek." (Psa. 27:8).

It is not enough for us to be alone with God; we must also be quiet. Job had much to say. There are forty-two chapters in the Book of Job.

It is full of words—many, many words. In chapter thirty-eight God speaks—then how quickly the book ends! So it is possible to be alone, intending to seek God, but to be so busy talking that we do not hear God. We complain to Him about other people, demanding that He rebuke them. We explain and defend our actions to Him, getting up from our knees without ever giving Him a moment in which to speak to us. Or we are so afraid God won't let us have our own way that we refuse to listen to Him. Many a man will justify himself into hell. When the Pharisee justified himself, God did not bless him (Luke 18). So many of us unintentionally follow his example. We try so very hard to prove to God that we are right that we are not quiet before Him.

If you go to your pastor with a problem, you plan to stay long enough to listen to his advice. When you go to God, set aside enough time to quiet your heart and listen. To obtain the greatest blessing from our private worship, we must cease our excuses and explanations and listen to Him. He may condemn, but more often He will cheer and encourage—if we are still.

"The wings of thy work, the wings of thy will, the wings of thine inmost longings, the wings of thy cherished desire—let them down," is the way

Amy Carmichael, missionary to the temple children of India, expresses the true attitude of prayer.

John Nelson Hyde was such an outstanding man of prayer that he became known as Praying Hyde. Dr. Wilbur Chapman, telling of meeting him, said that he asked, "Mr. Hyde, I want you to pray for me." Then he continues: "He came to my room, turned the key in the door, and dropped on his knees, and waited five minutes without a single syllable coming from his lips. I could hear my own heart thumping and beating. I felt hot tears running down my face. I knew I was with God. Then, with upturned face, down which tears were streaming, he said, 'O God.' Then, for five minutes at least, he was still again; and then, when he knew that he was talking with God, there came from the depths of his heart such petitions for me as I had never heard before. I rose from my knees to know what real prayer is."

We may do less, but we shall accomplish more if we spend time with God. "The Father seeketh such to worship him" (John 4:23).

I John 3:16

Lord give me love, the love that Jesus had
When here on earth, for all that flocked Him round
For any cause. He loved them, though He found
Some set against Him,—loved them, good or bad.
Had I this love, 'twould be my joy to sound
Thy praises forth, whereas my heart is sad
To find it duty. And exceeding glad
Would be my aim, where sin and death abound,
To seek the lost, and, scorning curse and threat,
Win them to Thee. But, oh! my Lord, as yet
I dare not venture, for I fear them so.
Oh! give me love, that I may self forget,
Nor courage need. Fill me to overflow
With Thy great love, whose depth no man can know.

H. K. Bentley

6

Prayer for Others

"Brethren, pray for us."—II Thessalonians 3:1

"PLEASE PRAY FOR ME." "Please pray for my son." "Please pray for my Sunday school class." "Please pray for the young Chinese believers." "Please pray that we may reach the Lisu tribes people."

So the requests come, one after another, day after day. Our hearts, full of love, respond. We want to pray, and we want to pray effectively; so we start the long road of learning to pray for others.

Many of us, when we pray, still retain our childish way of praying, "Lord, bless So-and-so." This may be all right if we understand what is meant when we speak thus and keep the true meaning of the word "bless" in mind.

When you ask the Lord to bless the non-Christian, you are asking Him to bless them in turning away every one of them from his iniquities. There is no other way the Lord could bless the person who is not His child. And when you pray God to "bless" the Christian, you are not praying that the Lord will prosper him materially, but that he will lead a life of obedience, for in Deuteronomy 28, where a long list of blessings is recorded, all of them rest on obedience.

To ask the Lord merely to bless our friends, however, is praying second-best, because the Lord said, "*What* wilt thou have me to do?" and He is still asking us to be definite in our prayers, not only for ourselves, but also for others.

"Pray in a business-like fashion, earnestly, definitely, statedly," is the way Mary Slessor, missionary to Africa, asked her friends to pray for her.

Use a section of your devotional notebook for your prayer list. You have heard missionaries say, "Please put me on your prayer list." Be assured they mean it. Paul must have had a prayer list to remember all the people for whom he said he prayed. We human beings forget too easily.

Outstanding men of God have found that they have to have a prayer list. J. O. Fraser, who went to the Lisu tribes in southeast China, said,

"I also find it helpful to make a short list, like notes prepared for a sermon, before every season of prayer. The mind needs to be guided as well as the spirit attuned. I can thus get my thoughts in order and, having prepared my prayer, can put the notes on the table or chair before me, kneel down and get to business."

You will probably find that there are so many who need prayer that you will not be able to pray for them all every day. You might have to have a different list for each day. For instance, pray on Monday for those who need Jesus. On Tuesday, pray for your friends. On Wednesday, pray for that part of the world called the "home field." On Thursday, pray for the part which is called the "foreign field."

On Friday, pray for your own church, from the cradle roll through each department to the minister. On Saturday, pray for those who don't fit into the other lists, for those like your former Sunday school pupils.

Head each day's list with an appropriate verse. For Sunday you might use, "This is the day which the Lord hath made; we will rejoice and be glad in it" (Psalm 118:24). On this day, instead of asking for anything, just praise Him for His goodness and rejoice in His love. For Monday's list of unsaved, you might use, "The

Lord is not slack concerning his promise, as some men count slackness; but is long-suffering to us-ward, not willing that any should perish, but that all should come to repentance" (II Peter 3:9). You will often cling to this verse, as some names remain on the unsaved list year after year!

We should be especially vigilant in praying for our own unsaved loved ones. Too often, because they are our loved ones and we know their good qualities, we hope they will slip into heaven somehow, and we grow lax in our prayers. If you have a deep conviction of sin and of their need of Christ, you will pray night and morning until God saves them.

In praying for the same people, it is easy to fall into a rut and pray for the same things; so, instead of asking the Lord each day to save these people, suppose you pray around their lives, for their friends, their work, their home life. And when you transfer one of these to Tuesday, how your heart will rejoice since they have become Christians!

For Tuesday, you might use the reminder, "Pray one for another" (James 5:16). This is a solemn trust and the test of how much you really think of your friends. It is also helpful to place special verses after as many names as possible.

You want the time you spend in prayer to count; therefore, you should pray according to Scripture. You will have greater faith in your prayers if you find a verse which indicates that your prayers are in the will of God.

Why pray for *things* for your friends? It is true that many people consider the blessing of the Lord to be either the acquisition of things or the escaping of trouble, but it is much more than that. God does supply the material needs of the just and the unjust alike. The far greater need for all of us is the spiritual. How must it sound to God, who hears all prayers, if we ask continually for *things?* So your friends, if you pray according to scripture, will receive the material things they need plus the spiritual things for which you have prayed.

For the one who has not been a Christian long, you might pray that he may "grow in grace and in the knowledge of our Lord and Saviour, Jesus Christ" (II Peter 3:18). One model prayer is this: "that he would grant you, according to the riches of his glory, to be strengthened with might by his Spirit in the inner man; that Christ may dwell in your hearts by faith; that ye, being rooted and grounded in love, may be able to comprehend with all saints what is the breadth, and length, and depth, and height; and to know the love of Christ, which passeth knowledge, that ye might be filled with all the fulness of God" (Ephesians 3:16-19). Or, "And this I pray, that your love may abound yet more and more in knowledge and in all judgment; that ye may approve things that are excellent; that ye may be sincere and without offense till the day of Christ; being filled with the fruits of righteousness, which are by Jesus Christ, unto the glory and praise of God" (Philippians 1:9-11).

We have mentioned before about praying according to the Scriptures, but I cannot emphasize too strongly the need of prayer that is guided by the revealed will of God. This alone can give you confidence that your prayers will be answered. "And this is the confidence that we have in him, that, if we ask anything according to his will, he heareth us" (I John 5:14).

On Wednesday, which you might take to pray for the home field, you might remember this Scripture, "For I was an hungred, and ye gave me meat: I was thirsty, and ye gave me drink: I was a stranger, and ye took me in: I was in prison, and ye came unto me" (Matthew 25:35, 36). Prayer is one way of obeying these words. You may not be able to go at all; but you can pray for the churches in the rural districts, for the missionaries in Kentucky among the mountain folks and for those in hospitals and jails.

Thursday might be your day to pray for the foreign field. A good verse to use is, "Withal praying also for us, that God would open unto us a door of utterance" (Colossians 4:3). Those who go need our backing. There is a story told of a young missionary whose church promised to pray for him when he went to the field. Though he worked hard in his service far from home, he felt himself a failure. Furlough time came; and he went home, slipping quietly into the first home church prayer meeting after his arrival. Not one voice was raised in prayer for him and his work that evening, and then he realized why his term as a missionary had seemed so hard and why he had felt himself a failure.

A North China missionary wrote in desperation "Please tell me, is *anyone* praying for me?" Another missionary wrote, "We have enough money for our work, but we need prayer that we may have conversions."

A missionary on furlough, hearing the few prayers for other missionaries, remarked, "It discourages me to think that this is all the prayer backing I will have when I return to the field."

Unless you have been in a position of attack

by the enemy, you do not know how frantic a person can become in his need of prayer. Prayer becomes the most important thing in the world. The missionary goes into the strongholds of Satan, and only prayer will win the battle. He desperately needs your prayer help.

You may be unable to go "unto the uttermost part of the earth," but your prayers most certainly can go.

It is your Christian privilege to have missionary fellowship all over the world. If a missionary goes out from your church, adopt him. A friend of mine left a church with a membership of 5000 to go to the field. When she returned, six years later, only one person in that church was still writing to her!

If you hear a missionary speaker, adopt him. Perhaps your more missionary-minded friends can suggest a missionary to you, or you can secure a list of missionaries from the missionary society of your church. You can write either to the mission board of your denomination or to a faith board; either will gladly send you the name of a missionary. Mission boards know the value of prayer and do everything they can to stimulate prayer.

After you have selected your missionary, then "add to your faith—knowledge." Learn all you can about the missionary, the country in which he is serving, and his problems. If you can get a picture of him, hang it in a conspicuous place in the kitchen or the bedroom, wherever you will see it oftenest and be reminded most frequently to pray for him.

We take our conveniences so much for granted. It may surprise you to learn the inconveniences of the different countries. There are neither tomatoes nor ice cream in China. In Mongolia, the missionary must live in a tent. There is no day of rest in India, except where the Cross has gone. Mail reaches Point Barrow, Alaska, but twice a year; and in some places in Africa, it is quite cold.

Write to your missionary, and ask to be put on the circular letter list. Most missionaries do not have the time to write many or frequent letters, but send carbon copies of a letter to their different friends and prayer helpers. Or sometimes they write this general letter to a friend or relative at home who takes the responsibility of retyping or mimeographing it and sending it on to interested and praying friends. Some missionaries write such a letter once a month; others every three months; and still others, only every six months.

Most mission boards put out a monthly pamphlet or magazine with articles about the different parts of the field. Either the letter or the magazine will keep you informed of the needs of the field so that you may pray definitely and effectively.

Here is a list of things for which to pray for the missionaries. (It was suggested by Mr. and Mrs. Allyn Cooke, missionaries to the Lisu in southeast China.)

I. Spiritual life
  a. Their spiritual growth
  b. Their prayer life

Spiritually the missionaries give out daily and need constant refreshing; yet they have very little Christian fellowship. Often they are the only Christians for hundreds of miles. Think of the steadfast faith needed to be the only believer among thousands of heathen!

II. Health
  a. Their general health
  b. Their mental health

Missionaries undergo a greater physical strain than the average person because of the abrupt changes in climate, the strange food, and the unsanitary habits of the heathen. Pray that they may be kept from having colds. You know how your work is neglected if you have a cold, and the same is true on the mission field. Often the missionary lives in a house which is not properly heated or among natives who do not understand how easily germs are scattered. Prayer lightens all these conditions. And pray for the protection of the minds of missionaries, that these workers in foreign places may not become morbid or morose or allow their constant contact with native life to undermine their spiritual convictions. Then there is the strain of knowing that the eternal destiny of those about them may depend upon them and the strain of living under the constant watchful eyes of the natives.

III. Wisdom
   a. What to do
   b. When to do it
   c. What not to do
   d. Where to go

Usually the missionary is the only Christian for miles. He sees hundreds of souls without Christ. The needs are so great and lie in so many directions that he cannot reach them all. It takes wisdom to know *where* to preach.

IV. Material needs
   a. Food
   b. A suitable place to live

c. Means of travel
d. Literature

Financially, missionaries have not only the average needs, but also the need for money, for Bibles, for churches and hospitals, for caring for the destitute, and for medicine.

V. Study
a. Time and inclination
b. Language mastery
c. Lessons and messages

If you consider how many things interrupt and interfere with your quiet time, you have a slight conception of the daily battle missionaries must fight, not only to have a quiet time, but also to study; and again, not only to study the message they must bring, but also to learn the language in which they must speak it.

VI. Contacts
a. With the authorities
b. With other missionaries
c. With the unsaved
d. With the Christians

You know that the authorities often misunderstand the missionaries' motives and put obstacles in their way, but you probably wonder why you have to pray for the relationship among missionaries. Consider for a moment—are you congenial with every Christian that you know? And while you know that the unsaved delight in finding fault with the Christian, you must also remember that after the native has become a Christian, he has still much to learn; so you must continue to pray for the relationship between the missionary and the Christians.

VII. Helpers
   a. God's choice of help in the home and in the church
   b. A real missionary vision for the helpers

Extend your prayers to the natives, that they may be converted and that they may live consistent Christian lives. They are used to the low standards of heathendom and are often loath to give up their heathen practices. It is also trying for them to take a stand against their friends and relatives. Some, indeed, face intense persecution. Pray that they may have the desire and the courage to win their friends and relatives to Christ. All too often the natives, like ourselves, desire the forgiveness of sins that is found in the Cross, but shrink from telling others of Him. Also since the heathen is often prejudiced against a "foreign" missionary, the best way for him to be won is by the other native converts.

VIII. Correspondence
   a. That contact be maintained with the home helpers
   b. That nothing be lost or stolen en route

You can help answer the first prayer by writing to the missionaries. Mail means a great deal to them in their isolation. They will understand if you do not have much to say; but they would appreciate even a card saying, "I am still praying for you."

On Friday you might pray for the home church, and a good verse to use in that connection is, "Help those women which labored with me in the gospel, with Clement also, and with other my fellow-laborers" (Philippians 4:3). Since the church is the instrument which God uses most often to help people find Christ, the devil is always trying to undermine the reputation of those who work in it. The Christian should consider it his duty to pray for the workers of the church in which God has placed him. He should pray not only for their teaching, but also for their preparation and their conduct.

On Saturday you might pray for people who did not fit into the other days, people who would come under the heading of "God forbid that I should sin against the Lord in ceasing to pray for you" (I Samuel 12:23). Perhaps these would be people whom you seldom see, and yet for whom you feel you should continue to pray.

The suggestions I have made about the different days are not to be considered a set rule. This is only a general plan to encourage you to widen your prayer vision.

Prayer must be under the guidance of the Holy Spirit, for we "know not what we should pray for as we ought; but the Spirit itself maketh intercession for us . . . " (Romans 8:26). It is convenient to keep a prayer list in a *looseleaf* notebook so it can be changed as the Spirit leads. Sometimes the Spirit will move you to take a person off your list. Even though that person's life does not give you assurance, He may give you assurance in your spirit. At other times, He may tell you something to do for some person for whom you are praying.

You will notice that we have not set aside a day for your family. Christ said, "Whosoever shall do the will of my Father which is in heaven, the same is my brother, and sister, and mother" (Matthew 12:50). When we come to God, we do well to give everyone and everything the value He would give. You could divide your family among others. If they are unsaved, they may be put with the unsaved. If they are Christians, they may be put with your Christian friends. If they serve the Lord, they may be considered with the Lord's other servants in the church, in the home field or in the foreign field.

If you pray for another Christian, let him know. It will encourage him to realize that someone is praying for him. You may think, because of the passage in Matthew where we are told to pray in secret, that we should not tell people we pray for them; but there are other Scriptures which incidate that we should. It is true that the Christian will not be showy about prayer, but it is a kindness to let others know that you pray for them. Sometimes people feel discouraged until they know someone is praying. We have an example in the Lord's telling Peter, "I have prayed for thee, that thy faith fail not."

There are a few more commandments about prayer to which I should like to draw your attention. Jesus said, "Pray ye therefore the Lord of the harvest that he will send forth labourers into his harvest" (Matthew 9:38). This is as much a commandment as that which says not to steal. The fields are white unto harvest. The cry for leaders, from Sunday school teachers to missionaries, is heard from every quarter. The least we can do is to pray unto the Lord of the harvest to thrust forth the needed laborers. If you know a young person whom you think the Lord could use, I suggest that you pray for that young person by name, that the Lord will thrust him forth.

Another verse to remember is, "My heart's desire and prayer to God for Israel is, that they might be saved" (Romans 10:1). Let us be constant in our prayers for the salvation of the Jew. If we do not know a Jew by name, we can make a general petition; but if we do know one or two Jews, we should make them our special burden.

There is every reason to be encouraged to pray for the conversion of God's ancient people. The American Board of Missions to the Jews says, "Jewish conversions are phenomenal, for God's conditions always work. The actual ratio of Jewish converts as compared to heathen converts is 7 to 2! These figures take into account the proportionate populations of the Jews and Gentiles and their expenditures for missions."

Yet another prayer command is, "I exhort, therefore, that, *first of all,* supplications, prayers, intercessions, and giving of thanks, be made for all men; for kings, and for all that are in authority; that we may lead a quiet and peaceable life" (I Timothy 2:1,2). Scripture does not tell us to pray for peace, but for the leaders that we may have peace. Our prayers should include the President, the Senators, the Representatives, the

Supreme Court judges, the local magistrates, and many others, all the way down to the sheriff. They need to be surrounded by prayers. Prayer is the cure for petty politics, for bribery, for lobbying.

We should pray for the leaders, whether we like them or not. The early Christians were instructed to pray for despots like Nero. If you love your country, don't criticize it; instead, pray for the leaders, ever remembering that "the most High ruleth in the kingdom of men, and giveth it to whomsoever he will" (Daniel 4:25).

Family Prayers

You say you are "busy this morning
In the maelstrom of family cares,
And someone must rush to the office,
So there isn't a moment for prayers."

Then the children are sent to the school-room,
And the grind of the day thus begins,
With no word from God's Book to remember,
Nor the echo of strengthening hymns.

What wonder the burdens are heavy,
And the hours seem irkesomely long!
What wonder that rash words are spoken,
And that life seems discordant and wrong!

And at even, discouraged and wearied,
You carelessly go to your rest,
Forgetting that Jesus is waiting
To pillow your head on His breast.

He longs for a word of thanksgiving,
And to hear your love spoken again;
He asks to review the day's record,
And to cleanse it of blotches and stain.

But if you forget Him so often,
Sometime you may knock at His gate,
And awaiting the summons to enter,
You may hear, "You are praying too late."

So pause for a little each morning,
And again at the close of the day,
To talk with the Master who loves you—
Remember, He taught us to pray.

—LAURA HUBBARD JACCARD

7

Family Prayers

"As for me and my house, we will serve the Lord."
—Joshua 24:15

ONE SUMMER my husband and I went visiting relatives. It was a pleasant surprise to go into home after home and see that they held family prayers. I think it would surprise all of us if we knew how many homes across the length and breadth of the United States have family prayers. It isn't a thing one goes around talking about—but it is done!

If your family isn't used to having them, you will not find them as difficult to begin as you think. If you are one of the younger members of the family, it might be well first to go to your mother or your father to ask for help. If, however, you are one of the older young people or one of the parents in the home, you might well, after breathing a little prayer to God for help, say aloud, "Don't you think we ought to pray together each day?"

Your family may look surprised and may even demand a reason for your suggestion. Now it is for you to straighten your shoulders, smile your most appealing smile, and reply, "We're united in everything else; why not in our prayers to God?" They will probably agree to try family prayers, and that is when your battle will really begin. Everyone is so busy.

In this day when the prophecy, "Many shall run to and fro and knowledge shall be increased" (Daniel 12:4), is being fulfilled, it is difficult to persuade people to stop long enough even to realize that they are only going around in circles. And they will continue to go round and round until they practice waiting on God. "They that wait upon the Lord shall renew their strength; they shall mount up with wings as eagles; they shall run, and not be weary; and they shall walk, and not faint" (Isaiah 40:31).

Once you have gained your family's consent, select the time which is most convenient. After a meal—breakfast or dinner—is usually best. You will find the new habit difficult to form. There will be times when every member of the family thinks he has a good excuse for not staying for devotions. That is because "we wrestle not against flesh and blood, but against principalities, against powers, against the rulers of the darkness in this world, against spiritual wickedness in high places" (Ephesians 6:12).

Satan will try to discourage you, to make you think you can't succeed. But if everyone leaves, hold the devotions by yourself. Remember that the Word is the "power of God unto salvation" (Romans 1:16) and doggedly continue. In time your very faithfulness will win your family.

In discussing family devotions, it would be easy merely to tell a person to read the Bible and pray. But you need to use wisdom in selecting what you will read and in deciding for what you will pray. Here are a few suggestions for the Bible reading.

Many devout families read and reread only their favorite passages of Scripture. We need the full revelation of God from cover to cover.

You should plan to read the Bible through in family worship; but it is best to read the New Testament first, because more people are acquainted with it and people enjoy hearing that about which they know something. The Psalms might be read next and finally the Old Testament.

The first time you read the Old Testament, I suggest that you skip any chapter which does not hold your family's interest, such as the genealogies and the description of the Tabernacle furniture. Many a girl or boy has started to read the Bible and hasn't gone beyond Exodus because he did not understand the symbolism in it and thought it dry. You wouldn't want this to happen in your family.

Paul fed only milk to the babes in Christ. As your family grows spiritually, they will want to hear each "jot and tittle." Remember that "All scripture is given by inspiration of God, and is profitable for doctrine, for reproof, for correction, for instruction in righteousness" (II Timothy 3:16). In other words, while all is inspired, it is not all written for the same purpose. Some passages may be more fitting for family worship than others.

Instead of having one person always read the Scripture, why don't you have each member take a turn? That will help them all to acquire a Scriptural vocabulary, and they will not be embarrassed if sometime they are asked to read the Bible in public.

Along with the Bible, some families use a devotional guide. An older Christian will be glad to help you select one. For the average family, these guides are of value. They are gauged to the spiritual depth of the average person and point out truths that he would not observe for himself.

As you go on with the Lord, however, you will find that much in them is surface truth and you will instinctively seek something deeper. You may have to satisfy this urge in your private devotions; but if you are fortunate enough to have a family who grows with you, you will want to use a devotional book.

The books are usually deeper than the booklets. The very fact that they are printed in the more permanent form shows that at least the publisher thought they were of more lasting value.

Among the better known devotional books are *My Utmost for His Highest* by Oswald Chambers, the *With Christ* series by Andrew Murray, *Streams in the Desert* by Mrs. Cowman. There are others which may be bought in any Christian book store; they are also listed for purchase in Sunday school literature. While the Bible is sufficient for all our needs, it is true that these writers have prayed, and the Lord has revealed rich secrets to them. Their books throw a light upon Scripture which we might not see.

No matter which you use—devotional guide or book—it will provide a means for someone else to take part in devotions. If you can manage the situation tactfully, it is good to have the one who needs the Scripture most read it. He will have to pay more attention if he does the reading.

Of course you will pray together. You may feel that, because you are with your own family, you are free to pray anything you wish. You are fortunate if that is true of your family; but in most families even our prayers will, out of Christian love, have to be gauged by the spiritual depth of the weakest member.

Any family should be spiritual enough to thank God for His goodness and to ask guidance in daily life; at first, perhaps, there will be no more than that. In time, however, most families broaden their viewpoint by including others in the prayer, not only friends and the sick, but also the work of missionaries and other specific needs. Lead them onward step by step in prayer.

If it is at all possible, persuade each member of the family to pray. Help them to find their voices for the Lord. "Whosoever therefore shall confess me before men, him will I confess also before my Father which is in heaven" (Matthew 10:32). Explain to them that a spirit of thankfulness is more important than the length of the prayer. Encourage them to say even an audible "Thank Thee, Lord." Suggest that they ask,

"Lord, teach me to pray," and He most certainly will answer. But if they can find their voices no other way, you might repeat the Lord's prayer together.

Encourage them to pray, but do not insist. After all, prayer is to God and is sacred. One cannot force it, any more than one would force the opening of a rosebud.

Be sure to include the children in your family worship. A baby should be so young when he begins to attend that he doesn't remember the first time any more than he remembers the first time he ate. A friend of mine, a widow with five children, said that when she knelt to pray, her baby used to toddle over to her and cuddle beside her. Sometimes he even crawled over her feet. She didn't scold the boy, for she explained, "I want his earliest memory to be of his mother kneeling in prayer."

When children are present at the devotional time, it should be lighter. For instance, you might read a book of Bible stories written especially for children. But be sure to read a few verses directly from the Scripture so that they will learn Bible phraseology and have them learn a short memory verse and join in prayer.

If you have a piano in your home, you are fortunate; but if you don't, sing anyway. Some like to open and close the devotions with a hymn. If someone can pitch the tune, that is fine; but if not, anyone can "make a joyful noise unto the Lord." Jesus and His disciples sang at the Last Supper. Scripture says, "And when they had sung a hymn, they went out into the mount of Olives" (Matthew 26:30).

If the children ask questions, answer the questions. They may not seem important to you, but they may be of the utmost importance to the child. Little minds are deep, and they make decisions which shape their thinking for the rest of their lives.

If you do not know the answer to the question asked, promise to find out what it is. Most people ask what are called "stock questions." That means that other people have asked them before, and Christian books have been written with the answers. You can buy these books at your Christian bookstore or through the advertisements in your Sunday school papers, and they are worth your investment.

This may sound like work, but what of that? We are "workers together with God" and are instructed to be "workmen that need not to be ashamed."

Family worship need not take much time. If there are school children in the family, one has to get up only fifteen or twenty minutes earlier to have devotions before the children leave. And the day is started right for the entire family.

Making children aware of the presence of God is both important and easy. It is important because a knowledge of His presence will be a lifetime check on their actions, and it is easy if His presence is natural to you. Let them hear you offer a word of thanksgiving each morning. Accustom them to hearing audible prayer at any time of the day or night when there is need for prayer. Make His presence a reality to them, for He is there.

Perhaps your next question will be, should you have family worship when you have company? The answer is, most assuredly, yes.

Your home is your castle; and if guests are there at the usual time for family worship, you should invite them to join you. If they are Christians, they will be delighted. If they are not Christians, a glimpse into the secret of the Christian home may be a help to them.

The only change necessary would be to omit the more personal references in your prayers and to select the Scripture with care. "Be ye therefore wise as serpents and harmless as doves" (Matthew 10:16). Do not read a difficult doctrinal passage or a passage such as the one on a woman's having long hair, which might only start a discussion without benefit to their souls. Read some beautiful message, such as Psalm 103 or Isaiah 55 or John 14. Try to give your guests a longing to read the Bible for themselves.

In Everything Give Thanks

II Thessalonians 5:18

Give thanks! God's mercies manifold
Most gracious and abundant are,
Supplying to the mind and heart
The blessings which would life enrich:
Perhaps not wealth of lands or gold,
Which perish often in their use,
But tasks of worth to be performed,
Whose final fruitage rich should be—
The wish and will to love and serve,
A place wherein to play one's part,
That when the days have passed away,
And reckoning for them be made,
It will be counted quite enough,
If faithfulness has marked the way,
If whatsoever was the task,
The Master's glory was the goal.
Then thankful be, nor fear to tread
The unknown path which love directs,
Assured that God will ne'er forsake,
But true and constant e'er remain.

—Fred Scott Shepard

8

Table Grace

"He took bread, and gave thanks and brake it."
—Luke 22:19

A TWIN to family worship is grace. It is another way in which the family as a unit pauses to remember the Creator and Saviour and to thank Him for His goodness.

Jesus, the divine Son of God, said grace. At the feeding of the five thousand, "Jesus took the loaves, and when he had given thanks, he distributed to the disciples" (John 6:11). His example should be sufficient reason for anyone who loves Him.

Grace is the little Christian ceremony which distinguishes man from the animals. When food is put out for animals, the instinct is, except perhaps in the case of trained pets, to be the first and to eat the most. The slight waiting for others and the giving of thanks lifts man above the animals.

Some time when you are in a restaurant, watch the different people. When the non-Christian family sits down and food is brought, each one starts to eat without regard for the others. The Christian family, even though they may sometimes omit grace in public, usually automatically wait for one another.

It is best to say an impromptu grace, because that keeps it from becoming formal; but if you can't—the important thing is that you do say it! If a person is naturally shy and has never had the opportunity to overcome his shyness, it is better to say a memorized grace from the heart than to omit altogether the giving of thanks. It can be varied by learning a new grace from time to time. Even if you say the same petition each day, you can think of what you are saying and repeat it clearly and distinctly, praying not merely with the lips, but also from the heart.

Here are some forms of grace you might use. "Dear Lord, come and be our Guest; let the food we eat be blest." "For this and all Thy other gifts of grace, we give Thee thanks." Or, "We thank Thee, Lord, for this food. Bless it to our use and us in Thy service. In Jesus' name, Amen."

These are all brief because grace should be brief. It is only of value as long as those who listen give thanks too. At mealtimes people are hungry and the food is growing cold. Human nature is too frail to allow for long prayers before meals.

Usually the father, as the head of the house, asks the blessing. If the father is not a Christian, the mother may ask the blessing; but even a non-Christian should be grateful enough for food to give thanks to God.

If one of the formal graces is used, why not have the family say it together? Or you might take turns saying grace. This way it will become natural to all; and if one is asked to say grace in company or when away from home, he will not be self-conscious.

If for some reason the family does not all eat at the same time, those who eat alone should take a moment to bow their heads and thank the Giver of every good gift for the food.

The Early Morning Watch

"O Jehovah, in the morning shalt thou hear my voice; In the morning will I order my prayer unto thee, and will keep watch." Psalm 5:3

The birdies wake at peep of day,
And "Hallelujahs" raise;
They greet the dawn with carols gay,
And their Creator praise.

And little children too, are heard
In prattle sweet and clear;
The aged waken with the bird
When morning draweth near.

The Comrades of the Quiet Hour
Do rise betimes each day;
They know the need of grace and power
To tread the narrow way.

Does Holy Writ a story tell
Of worshipers at morn?
Aye, more than one, we know full well,
Rose e'er the day was born.

To offer prayer and sacrifice,
They rose before the light;
And women, virtuous and wise,
Rose oft, while yet 'twas night.

Wise seers and patriarchs, not few,
Ere dawn their altars raised;
And righteous kings, and psalmists too,
Sang early, "God be praised!"

Our Saviour, also, rose and sought
A solitary place,
Where He might meet, in sorrow fraught,
His Father, face to face.

Come, let us rise at morning light
And seek our God in prayer;
Praise Him who kept us through the night
And cast on Him our care.

—Pearle M. Sterling

9

Prayer Partners

"Strive together with me in your prayers to God."
—Romans 15:30

ONE OF THE GREATEST joys of prayer is having a prayer partner. Usually in a family there are many different degrees of spirituality, and the more devout person does not feel free to pray fully about everything on his heart. He yearns for someone with whom to pray, and a prayer partner with equal spiritual yearning is priceless.

There are strong promises for prayer partners to claim. "Again I say unto you, That if two of you shall agree on earth as touching any thing that they shall ask, it shall be done for them of my Father which is in heaven. For where two or three are gathered together in my name, there am I in the midst of them" (Matthew 18:19,20).

Time after time after I had asked someone to pray with me, I have been startled by the swiftness of the answer. Perhaps I had been struggling a long time; then someone prayed with me, and lo, the answer came.

Why not ask the Lord to send you a prayer partner? It may be a member of your family. It may be a friend. But whoever it is, you will find that praying with him will make this the most beautiful friendship in your life.

All of our friendships would be beautified by more prayer. There should be more spontaneous praying. When we discuss the problems of our friends, we ought to stop talking and pray. Prayer should be as natural among Christians as talking one to another.

So if God gives you a prayer partner, be informal if possible when you pray with him. Talk about something, pray about it, and then talk again.

It is said of D. E. Hoste, general director of the China Inland Mission from 1900 to 1935, that he would stop abruptly in the midst of prayer, make a note or two about something that had occurred to him, and then return to his praying. Or if a mid-morning cup of cocoa or tea were brought to him, he would courteously accept it and go on praying, taking occasional sips from his cup meanwhile.

He had learned the secret of accepting God's presence *all* the time.

If you cannot see your partner often, you might form the partnership anyway and telephone or even write each other, giving requests and comparing answers. This form of partnership is especially helpful in praying for a Sunday school class. Often a class is large, and there are many names to remember. You can give your friend half of the class as his prayer responsibility.

When the Lord has given you a prayer partner, watch out! Temptation always follows blessing. Immediately after the Lord was baptized, He was tempted by the devil; so after we have taken a step forward in the Lord, the devil tempts with ill will, tiredness, or with whatever sin it is that most easily besets us. He will try to break up the partnership if he can.

My Life

Psalm 27:1

At Thy dear feet, once pierced for me
With cruel nails upon the tree,
I lay my life for use by Thee;
Henceforth to know no anxious care.
With cheerful heart my load to bear,
My sole resort—believing prayer.

No worry, lest my work be stayed;
No hurry, lest I be delayed,
By haste—to prayerlessness betrayed;
Not careful to be praised of man,
But only to be taught Thy plan—
What Thou wilt have me do, I can.

No greed of gain, for Thou hast said
That if the beasts and birds are fed,
Thy children shall not lack for bread.
How sweet to live alone in Thee,
In danger to Thy wings to flee,
The name of Jesus all my plea!

Before Thee let Thy servant stand,
To watch Thine eye, Thy beckoning hand
And promptly move at Thy command.
So shall my life be one sweet day,
Lit up by heaven's cloudless ray,
A walk with God, a radiant way!

—A. T. PIERSON

10

The Secret of His Presence

"Pray without ceasing."—I Thessalonians 5:17

BROTHER LAWRENCE, a devout man of God who lived in the seventeenth century, learned so thoroughly the secret of praying without ceasing that his letters were collected into a book as an example for the rest of us. The book is called *The Practice of the Presence of God.*

When Brother Lawrence first served in the kitchen of the monastery, he disliked his work; but feeling that he should do everything for the love of God and with a prayer that he might do the work well, he found during the fifteen years he spent in the kitchen that everything was easy to do. He saw that God was as much in the kitchen as He was at the altar. He wrote, "The time of business does not with me differ from the time of prayer; and in the noise and clutter of my kitchen, while several persons are at the same time calling for different things, I possess God in as great tranquility as if I were upon my knees at the altar." That is the ultimate in Christian experience; and if he, a humble Christian in a monastery kitchen, could reach that place, so can you in your more pleasant surroundings.

May I suggest that, as a help toward this attitude, you do two things at the conclusion of your private devotions. Select a verse to memorize, and select someone or something to be a special object of prayer during the day.

Pick a verse from your promise box, so that you can keep it in your pocket and glance at it during the day, or copy one from your reading and carry it with you. If you ride to work, memorize it on the streetcar or bus. If you work at a machine, repeat it over and over again as you operate the machine. The noise will drown out what you are saying. If you work at a desk, place the card where your eyes will fall upon it at odd moments. If you are a housewife, put it over the sink and glance at it every time you turn the faucet. No one has a better opportunity to memorize Scripture than the housewife. She can repeat the verse over and over as she peels vegetables, irons, or runs the vacuum cleaner. And the message in the words will take the drudgery out of housework. "Oh, how love I thy law! it is my meditation all the day" (Psalm 119:97).

Decide also for whom you are going to pray, and ask the Holy Spirit to bring that person often to your memory during the day. Perhaps you will decide to pray for the tracts distributed among the Moslems. How great is the need for prayer behind the work among the Mohammedans! Or you might pray for the Nosu in China who are converted from rank heathendom. You may not know their names, but the Holy Spirit can use your prayer. Or perhaps you will decide to pray for a personal friend whose faith is weak or for someone who is going through deep waters. The decision is yours, but do decide upon something or some person. The needs are urgent.

In each of our lives there are many moments which might be turned into prayer times. What do you do when you wait for a streetcar or a bus? Do you fret, or do you pray? Prayer is "redeeming the time, for the days are evil" (Ephesians 5:16). All day long as people flit in and out of your mind, take their names to the Lord with a short petition for each. If someone telephones you, breathe a prayer for her as you replace the receiver. If someone writes you a special request for prayer, place the letter in a corner of your mirror; and every time your glance falls upon it, murmur a prayer. In front of your shorthand book or whatever tool you use often in your work, place the picture of a missionary; and every time you glance at the picture, pray.

And praise the Lord a thousand times a day. Every time you glance out the window at the flowers, the trees, and the birds, thank the Lord for the beautiful world in which you live. Every time you pick up something, thank the Lord for giving it to you. "Every good and perfect gift is from above and cometh down from the Father" (James 1:17).

These are but moments given to the Lord; but perhaps you can, like Francis Asbury, devote the first ten minutes of each hour to prayer. The first American Methodist bishop, he traveled an average of five or six thousand miles a year, going over all the newly settled country to preach. When he died, he was considered the best-known man in America; and more than twenty thousand people marched behind his coffin. As he traveled, he prayed for each Methodist preacher by name, until there were so many that it was humanly impossible to do so.

You may not be able every day to devote ten minutes of each hour to prayer; but if you believe prayer is important, you will do it whenever you can—for instance, when you are traveling, when you are on a vacation, or when you have free time on Sundays. Permit yourself the joy sometimes of spending extra time with the Lord. Refuse all invitations; even miss a meeting at church if necessary to spend that time alone with the Lord. How precious it is to give an evening to the Lord!

Or a whole day! Perhaps you have a cold and the doctor tells you to rest. You have often lamented, "I wish I had more time to read the Word!" Did you really mean it deep down in your heart? Then this is your opportunity to read a quantity of the Word. The day before Jonathan Goforth, missionary to China, went to be with the Lord, he asked his wife, "Please read to me the Gospel of John." He was blind and could not read it for himself. She read most of it to him. Jonathan Goforth was a man greatly used of God, not because he read a chapter of the Bible every day, but because his *desire* was to read a book a day. Jesus calls, "Come ye apart and rest awhile"; and your "off day" is your opportunity to answer His call.

The things you would like to do may tug at your heart for a moment. We are by nature an active race; but if we once learn to measure life in the light of eternity, we shall be thankful for these stops, because they mean time to devote to the Lord. "Delight thyself also in the Lord."

The work of the earth will crumble, but the quiet moments in which you learn to know God become a part of eternity.

Go to your room or even to bed with your Bible and your prayer list. You might add a Christian book, such as a volume of Spurgeon's sermons, or perhaps a Christian magazine. Completely relax, and "practice the presence of God."

After you have read a book or two of the Bible, take out your prayer list. Perhaps you have prayed faithfully each morning for those on it, but often you have had to pray hurriedly. Some mornings you had only time to say, "Lord, bless them." But on your day off you can take time really to pray for your relatives and friends, financially, physically, mentally, socially, spiritually—all the different things that you have wanted to pray. Let the Spirit of prayer pour through you for them.

Most of us are not used to long sessions of prayer, so if this idea of spending the day with God is new to you, try this: pray for one name; then rest a few minutes before you pray for the next friend. Suppose it does take a couple of hours, praying off and on, to remember all your friends, your neighbors, your pastor, the missionaries you know, and your relatives? You are in no hurry. God has taken you off life's treadmill so that you may spend a day in prayer.

There will be a temptation, especially the first two or three times you try this, to stop to read a secular magazine. Recognize the impulse for what it is, a temptation of the world to turn aside from God. Resist the devil and continue your spiritual meditations. Instead of the worldly magazine, no matter how interesting it appears, pick up a Christian book or booklet and read. Fellowship with the saints, listening to their words of testimony, will encourage your heart and strengthen your faith.

As the day wears on, an ecstacy, an inner glow, will gradually flood your being; then you will understand what the Scripture means when it says, "They that wait upon the Lord shall renew their strength."

Days like this will be few, it is true. Most of the time you will have to learn to include the Lord in the humdrum paths of life, but you can learn to do as Enoch did, to "walk with God" (Genesis 5:24) and to say with Israel, "I have seen God face to face" (Genesis 32:30).